Contents

Some words are shown in bold, **like this**. You can find out what they mean by looking in the glossary.

What is a habitat?

A **habitat** is a place where animals or plants live. An area covered in snow is a habitat.

Habitats provide food and **shelter** for the things that live there.

thick fur

Snowy habitats can be very cold.

Animals and plants have special features to live in the snow.

How do plants live in the snow?

Arctic poppies turn to face the sun whenever it appears. This helps them get the sunshine they need to make food and grow.

The petals of Arctic poppies make a cup shape. This shape helps them collect as much sunshine as possible.

Snowdrops can stay alive for a long time under snow. When the snow melts, they burst into bloom again.

Snowdrops have hard tips on their leaves to push through frozen soil.

Cushion plants, such as moss campion, look like cushions.

Their short leaves grow very close together. This helps protect them from cold weather.

The ground is often frozen in snowy **habitats**. This can make it hard for some plants to grow.

The roots of Arctic willows are very short and spread out sideways. Their short roots help them to grow in very thin layers of soil.

How do animals survive the cold in snowy habitats?

Collared lemmings dig burrows in the snow to stay warm. They line them with dry grasses, feathers and fur.

The collared lemming's front claws grow bigger for the winter to help it dig through snow and ice.

Ringed seals build snow caves above the ice where they and their babies can keep warm. They spend a lot of time in the water below the ice.

The seals have thick layers of blubber, or fat, which help keep them warm in the icy ocean.

Emperor penguins have blubber and thick coats of feathers to stay warm.

When it is very cold, emperor penguins huddle together. They take turns to be in the middle of the huddle where it is warmest.

Some animals survive the cold by **hibernating**. The Arctic ground squirrel hibernates for seven months a year.

Every two or three weeks, the Arctic ground squirrel shivers really quickly to heat up its body.

How do animals feed in the snow?

Snowy owls feed mainly on lemmings. Their excellent eyesight and hearing help them to find **prey** hidden in the snow.

Snowy owls can fly very quietly. When they spot prey, they fly down and grab it with their sharp **talons**.

A polar bear's favourite food is ringed seals. Its amazing sense of smell helps it to sniff out ringed seals under the snow.

Polar bears poke their heads in deep holes in the ice to search. Powerful jaws and claws help them to grab prey.

Reindeer feed on moss buried deep in the snow. Their large, wide hooves stop them from sinking as they search for food.

Reindeer also use their hooves to dig in the snow to uncover food.

hooves

Arctic wolves often hunt in packs. Together they can kill large **prey**, such as reindeer or musk oxen.

Arctic wolves have long, pointed teeth for grabbing and killing their prey. They also have wide, flat teeth to crush bones.

How do animals hide in the snow?

Arctic foxes need to hide from **predators**, such as polar bears and wolves. The colour of their fur helps them hide.

In winter, they have thick white coats to match the snow. When the snow melts in summer, their coats turn brown or grey.

Snow leopards live in snowy mountains. Their white, speckled fur helps them to stay hidden among rocks and snow.

Snow leopards stay hidden from **prey** by sneaking up on it from above.

How do animals protect themselves in the snow?

Walruses live on land and in the sea in snowy **habitats**. Their giant size helps to scare off most **predators**.

Walruses have long teeth called tusks, which they can use to protect themselves if predators attack.

tusks

Musk oxen use sharp horns on their heads to protect themselves against predators, such as wolves and polar bears.

When predators attack, musk oxen will form a circle around their young to protect them.

That's amazing!

Nose bot flies keep their babies warm by leaving them in the noses of reindeer.

The babies grow all winter and then get sneezed out in the spring!

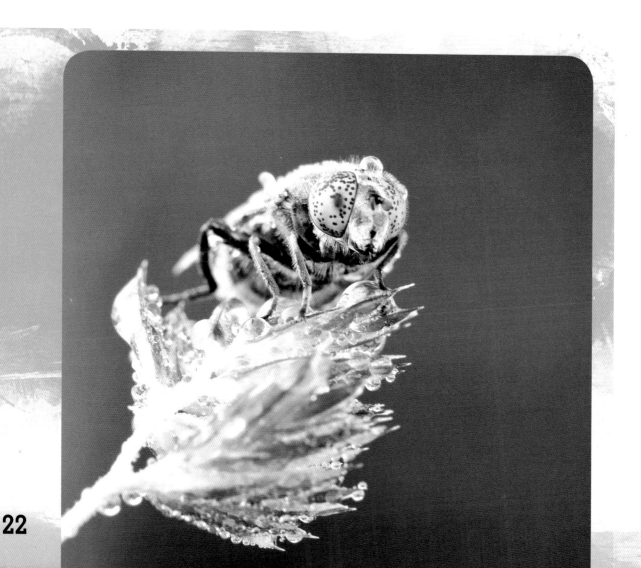

Picture glossary

 **habitat** a place where an animal or plant lives

 **hibernate** to sleep through the winter in a den or burrow to save energy

 **predator** an animal that hunts other animals for food

 **prey** an animal that is hunted by other animals for food

 **shelter** a place that protects from danger or bad weather

 **talon** the claw of a bird of prey

Find out more

Books

Katirgis, Jane. *Baby Snow Animals.* (Enslow Publishers, 2010)

Waldron, Melanie. *Polar Regions.* (Raintree, 2013)

Websites

http://kids.nationalgeographic.co.uk/kids/photos/arctic-animals
See more pictures and information on Arctic animals.

www.bbc.co.uk/nature/places/Arctic
Watch videos and look up profiles for Arctic animals.

Index